Robots

David Jefferis

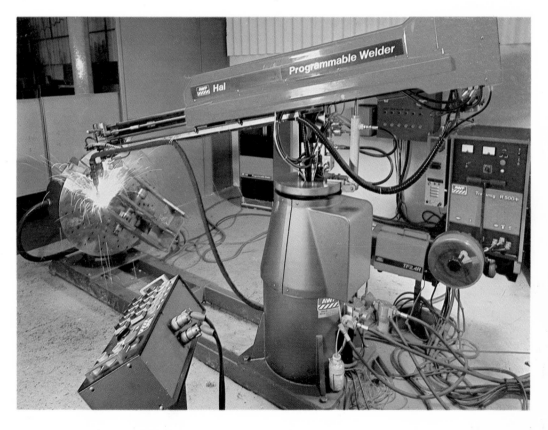

Franklin Watts
London   New York   Toronto   Sydney

© 1982 Franklin Watts Ltd
Reprinted 1983

First published in Great Britain in
   1982 by
Franklin Watts Ltd
12a Golden Square
London W1

First published in the USA by
Franklin Watts Inc.
387 Park Avenue South
New York
N.Y. 10016

UK ISBN: 0 85166 958 1
US ISBN: 0-531-04448-3
Library of Congress Catalog Card
   Number: 82-50066

Printed in Great Britain by
   Cambus Litho, East Kilbride

Illustrated by
Christopher Forsey
Hayward Art Group
Michael Roffe

Photographs supplied by
BBC
Fiat Auto UK Ltd
Hall Automation Ltd
Honeywell Information Systems
IBM UK Ltd
Lucas Films
MGM
National Film Archives
NASA
Space Frontiers Ltd
Sunday Times
Ian Wright

Technical consultant
Kenneth Gatland FRAS, FBIS

AN
EASY-READ
FACT
BOOK

Robots

Contents

What is a robot?

△ This 18th-century chess-playing "robot" defeated many human players. Its inventor opened the doors of the chest so that people could see inside. But it was later discovered that the chess pieces were moved by a man hidden inside the cabinet.

Robots are machines which can perform some of the actions of a person or animal. They are at work all around us, though few look like the popular idea of a robot – a gleaming metal and plastic mechanical man.

Robots come in all shapes and sizes, according to the job they are designed to do. A welding robot, for example, has only one arm. It does not need legs and feet to do its job properly.

People have been trying to build robots for centuries. A mechanical adding machine was made as long ago as 1642. This was the ancestor of today's computer. Lots of clever toys that looked like humans were made in the eighteenth century. Some could write letters, draw pictures and play musical instruments. But today's robots depend on one modern invention, the computer. This is the brain of a robot.

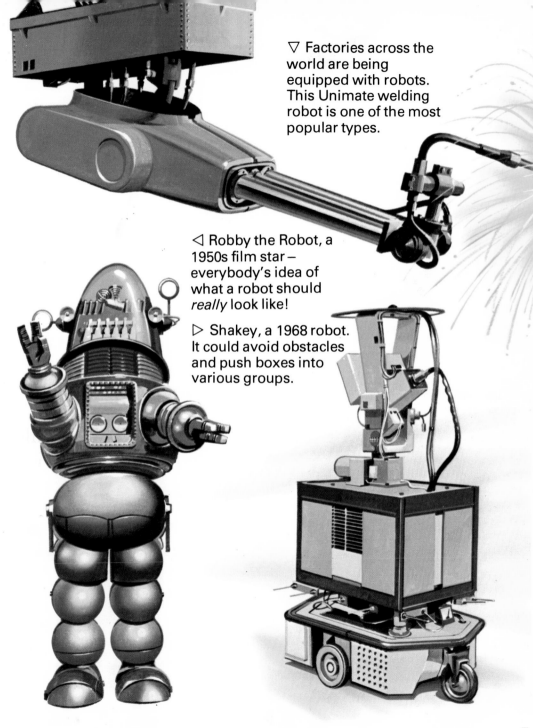

▽ Factories across the world are being equipped with robots. This Unimate welding robot is one of the most popular types.

◁ Robby the Robot, a 1950s film star – everybody's idea of what a robot should *really* look like!

▷ Shakey, a 1968 robot. It could avoid obstacles and push boxes into various groups.

5

The robot brain

△ Large computers like this look very impressive. But most of the equipment is needed for getting information in and out of the machine and for storage. The actual part used for computing is shrinking in size.

The brain of a robot is a small computer. Early computers were the size of a room and could perform only a few calculations a second. Modern ones are much smaller and can be millions of times faster.

At the core of a computer is a tiny microchip. Each chip is a complete electronic calculating circuit on a square of silicon (the "chip") a fraction of an inch across. Such chips are the brains which control millions of gadgets in everyday life – from calculators and digital watches to cameras and spy satellites. The small size and speed of microchips also make them ideal to control the actions of robots.

A robot is not intelligent by itself, and can perform only those tasks for which it is given a set of instructions, or program. A robot, unlike a human, cannot cope with the unexpected. If, for example, the car body for a weld-

Size of microchip

△ About 25 years ago, the computer able to match the calculating power in this tiny chip would have filled a large room.

◁ This picture shows a pocket calculator, with its electronic insides laid out on top. The microchip – which does all the hard work – is the small black square on the right. The rest of the workings consist of connections to the push buttons for our huge fingers to press.

ing robot does not appear at the right instant, the robot will simply weld into thin air.

As computer science advances, robots will get smarter. They will be able to tackle more and more complicated jobs in homes and factories.

Robot senses

Senses are as important to a robot as they are to a human. Touch is quite simple. Contact switches indicate when a robot hand moves up against something. Strain gauges can measure how hard it is grasping, so even massive steel fingers can gently grasp an egg without crushing it.

TV cameras are the eyes of a robot.

▷ This TV-eye view is what a Maverick missile (below) sees a few moments before it hits its target, a ship. The image has little detail, but there is enough for the missile's brain to tell that it is on target.

Just one may do, though several can be used if the robot has to view different parts of an object. The cameras do not have to be placed on the robot's "head." They can be fixed where they are most convenient, with cables joining them to the brain.

Microphones are robots' ears. There are already machines which can understand simple spoken commands, and robots can now speak as well. Soon, everything from cars to stoves will tell you how they are getting along with the job.

△ The Sharp EL-620 calculator speaks the numbers as you punch them out, then speaks the answer too. You still have to press the keys!

▽ A robot hand is very complicated. Pulleys, motors, rams and contact switches are all needed.

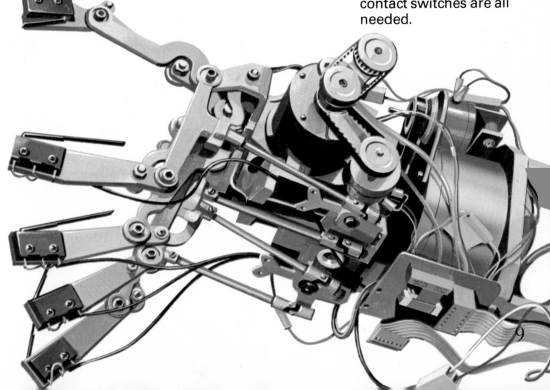

9

Made by robot

Robots are in the first stages of taking over the world's factories. The largest number work in the car industry. There they weld, paint and do various sorting jobs. Other things they make range from refrigerators to F–16 fighter jets.

Japan owns about three-quarters of the world's robots – about 80,000 – but sales are booming in other countries. Computers are expensive, often costing $100,000. But they are still selling because they work non-stop for 16 hours a day. They need no holidays or sick days, and can pay for themselves in two years or less.

A robot is not limited to just one job. It can be reprogrammed with a new set of instructions. In this way a robot that fills boxes one week may be sorting tins of tomatoes or loading packing cases on to a conveyor belt a week later.

△ The Unimate is one of the most widely used industrial robots. The hands can be easily changed from finger grippers to welding guns. Where floor space is tight, the Unimate can be slung from an overhead rack.

▷ A Unimate at work in a factory. This one is helping in the assembly of Fiat Strada passenger cars. The robots put the cars together more quickly and more precisely than the humans they have replaced.

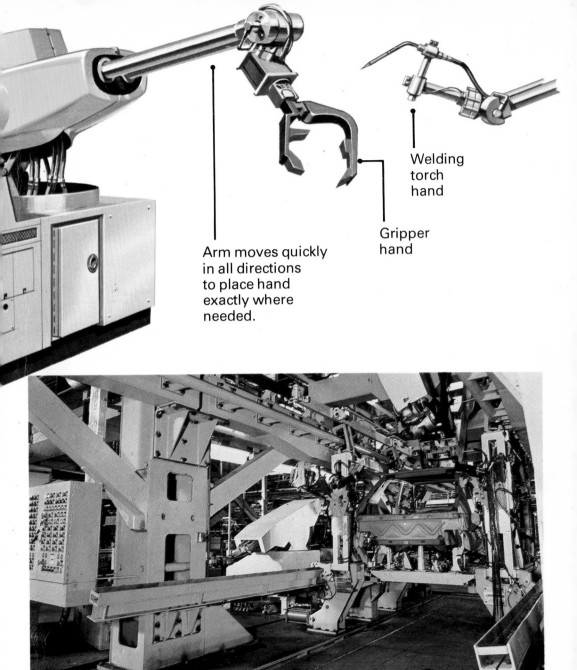

Welding
torch
hand

Gripper
hand

Arm moves quickly
in all directions
to place hand
exactly where
needed.

Danger! Robots at work

Remote-controlled robots are used in places too dangerous for humans.

The radioactive materials used in the nuclear industry give off radiation. This can cause illness or death. The first remote-controlled robots were made to handle such materials. The most common sort is a pair of arms. The operator sits safely behind lead-lined windows and moves a pair of hand grippers. A few feet away, in the "hot" area, another pair of grippers follows his movements exactly. In this way the most dangerous things can be handled in safety.

Another dangerous job is bomb disposal. The British Army sometimes uses robots to inspect booby traps.

In the future, robots may be clever enough to do jobs like this on their own. For the moment, a human operator is essential.

Camera

▷ The MOBOT not only has handling arms, but also can move around. Cameras give its operator a clear view of what is happening.

▷ This is a British Army bomb-disposal robot. It has cameras to inspect a bomb. A hammer can be fitted to break windows.

12

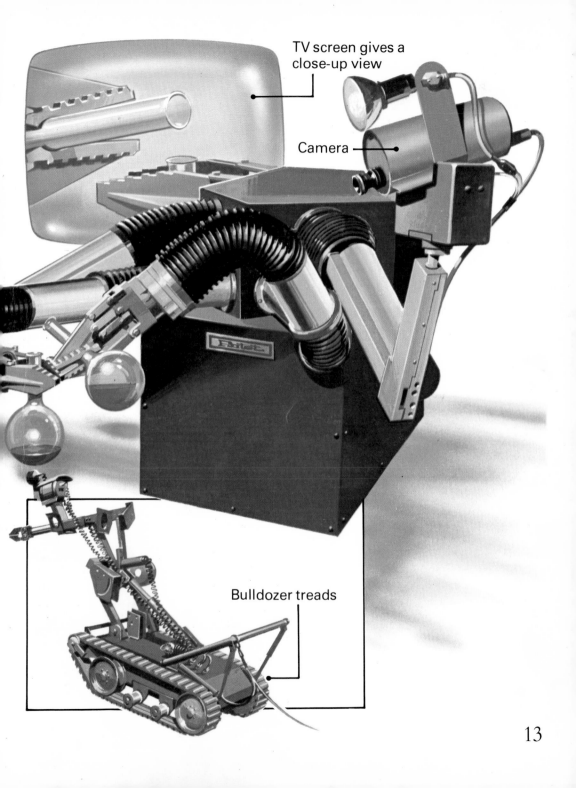

TV screen gives a
close-up view

Camera

Bulldozer treads

13

Robots on the roads

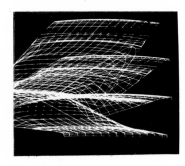

△ This is a computer drawing of a sports car hatchback window. Clever use of computers helps the designers make it thinner and lighter. Computers are used in all parts of car design, from engines to door frames.

Traffic controllers and car designers are using robots more and more.

Traffic in Tokyo is checked by 5,000 automatic detectors. Information is shown on a giant wall screen at traffic headquarters. Traffic jams are shown as lines of colored light. Buses and taxis can be rerouted to avoid jams.

Also in Japan, scientists are working on a robot replacement for the blind person's guide dog. Called the Meldog, the robot leads its master on preset routes. Each route has landmark points which are programmed into Meldog's memory. It rolls from point to point, avoiding obstructions like cars and trees. At each point it awaits a start signal to go along the next section of the route. As yet though, Meldog is no match for a friendly, faithful animal.

Car designers are including lots of robot equipment in their new models.

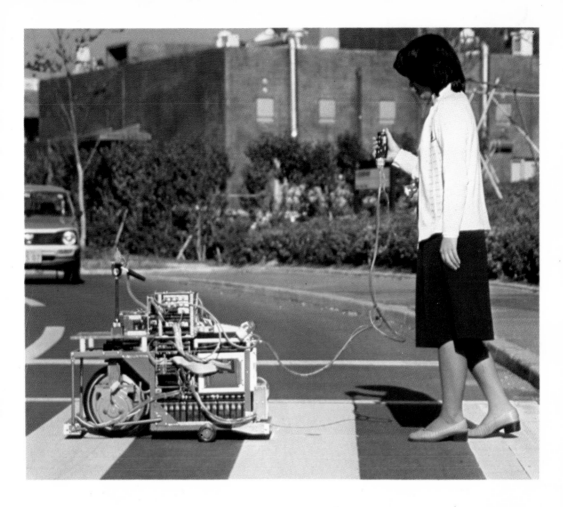

Many now have trip computers and speaking devices that give information about the car and the journey. A car fully controlled by robot does not yet exist, but if one is developed, human drivers – who make mistakes – could end up banned from the streets of tomorrow's cities.

△ Whirring quietly, the experimental Meldog leads a researcher across a pedestrian crossing. A hand control starts and stops the mechanical animal.

15

Underwater explorers

Robots that work in the underwater deeps come in many different forms.

There are mobile TV platforms and oil-rig inspection craft. A Japanese firm makes a robot bulldozer which can work 200 feet (60 m) below the surface. Russia uses underwater spy-eyes to check on the trawl nets slung below her fishing boats.

One of the most remarkable robots is the bottom lander. It collects samples of the odd potato-shaped manganese nodules which lie on the ocean floors. Some are rich in minerals and may be worth mining. Like a moonprobe, the lander drops down through the inky blackness of the Pacific Ocean. Once on the ocean floor, three scoops reach out to grasp nodules for the lander's computer-controlled test chambers.

When testing is over, the lander starts its long rise to the scientists in the research ship on the surface.

▷ This insect-like craft is typical of the many robots at work under the sea. This one has TV cameras, floodlights and big robot arms.

17

Space voyagers

In 1970, an eight-wheeled Russian mooncar was sent to explore the Moon's surface. It was a robot, operating under instructions sent by scientists working back on Earth.

Since then, robot explorers have visited most of the planets in the Solar System. Only the outermost worlds – Uranus, Neptune and Pluto – have yet to be examined in close-up.

Machines are better than men for long space trips. They are cheaper than manned craft and if something goes wrong with the mission, no astronauts are in danger.

Future robots include the Galileo probe. In 1984 it will parachute deep into the poisonous atmosphere of Jupiter. For further trips to Mars, a flight of "astroplanes" has been suggested. These flyers could cruise thousands of miles over the canyons and deserts of the red planet.

▽ A sunny day on Mars as shown by the cameras of the Viking spaceprobe in 1976. The pink sky took scientists by surprise. They had expected it to be dark blue. The planet appears to be lifeless.

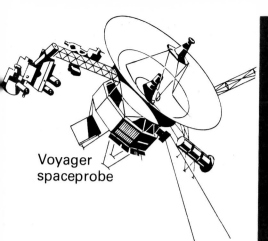

Voyager
spaceprobe

△ Voyager spaceprobes
have photographed
Jupiter and Saturn. In
1980 the delicate beauty
of Saturn's rings were
revealed by photos like
the one on the right.

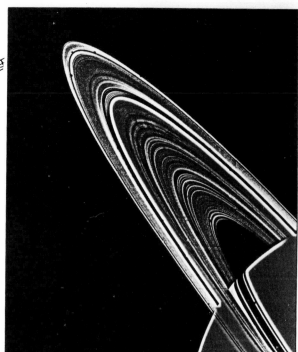

Fantasy robots

△ A Dalek from the British TV series *Dr Who*. These evil creatures constantly scheme to rule the universe.

Science-fiction movies have made robots familiar to everyone.

Robby the Robot starred in the 1950s film *Forbidden Planet*. He was the perfect butler and was programmed never to hurt a human.

HAL 9000, the computer in charge of the spaceship *Discovery*, went to the other extreme. In *2001, A Space Odyssey*, HAL took over the ship and killed all but one of the crew. The surviving astronaut managed to switch HAL off before the computer could kill him too.

The superstars of the robot world are C3PO and R2D2 of *Star Wars*. This pair shows two very different robot shapes and functions. C3PO is bronze-plated, but is human in shape and speaks excellent English. Little R2D2 is a mobile tin can. It talks in a mysterious machine-language of whistles, warbles and beeps.

△ An android blows a fuse in the film *Westworld*. Android is the name given to a robot built to look like a human.

◁ C3PO and R2D2. Despite their metal form, they are more popular than the human actors. Like other movie robots, they are operated by people hidden inside them.

Robots that walk

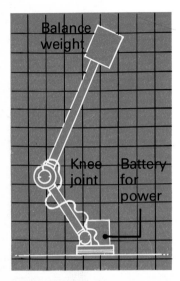

Balance weight

Knee joint

Battery for power

△ This blueprint shows an experimental robot leg being tested in the USA. It is learning to hop. Once it can do this well, a pair of legs will be joined together to make a walking and running version.

Science-fiction robots walk on their two legs with ease, but in real life walking is not so easy. Making a robot which can stand up and walk on smooth surfaces is not difficult. But the problems of coping with sudden changes in speed and direction have not yet been solved. Today's robots would fall over too easily.

For most jobs, two legs are not necessary anyway. On smooth surfaces, wheels are better and caterpillar tracks can take care of soft ground. Because legs would be very useful for climbing stairs or moving over rough ground, walking robots may be developed for such jobs.

The cargo carriers shown on the right are one solution to the balance problem. With four legs to carry them, such machines could gallop along smoothly and quickly.

▽ These cargo walkers are strolling through terrain which is ideal for them – swamp, river and rough ground. The walkers have a flexible eye stalk for TV vision and Unimate arms to load and unload.

Robots at home

△ Computers like this are becoming as popular in the home as hi-fi and video. The Sinclair ZX 81 is one of the simplest home computers.

The list of robot devices in the home gets longer every day. Familiar microchip-controlled gadgets include stoves and washing machines.

Next comes the powerful home computer, your robot overseer. A sudden change in the weather and it will adjust the heating to match. A loose roof tile will trigger a warning. If you are out, the computer may contact a repairman for you. Burglaries will be reduced as the computer will protect your home with sensitive detection instruments. The computer may recognize your fingerprints if you press a front door plate, making keys a thing of the past.

You will be able to instruct the computer by using your TV with a keyboard attached. More expensive models may be able to understand your speech and talk to you without a keyboard.

▷ Robot butlers may be in our homes within ten years, performing very simple jobs. Legs may be available, but butlers with wheels will be more likely.

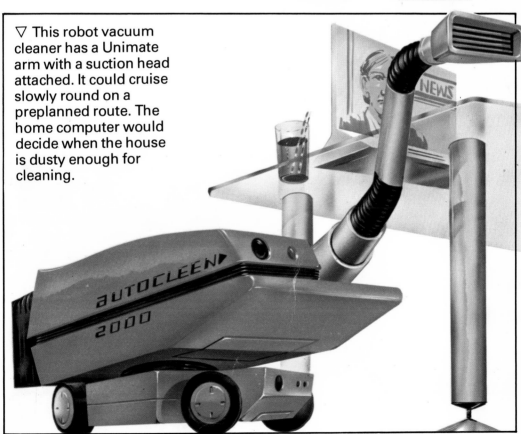

▽ This robot vacuum cleaner has a Unimate arm with a suction head attached. It could cruise slowly round on a preplanned route. The home computer would decide when the house is dusty enough for cleaning.

Robot warriors

Here you see a battlefield of the near future. In the front is a Mini-Missile. The MM is barely a yard long, but guided by its robot brain, can find its way to within feet of the target. The MM's small size and coating of radar-proof material make it almost impossible to detect or shoot down.

The strange spiky plane is an E55

△ A 1953 idea of what robot soldiers might look like. In fact, no commander would want tall, shiny, easily spotted tin men. They could be destroyed too easily.

①

26

Superfly. It is piloted by remote control. It can also listen to the enemy's radio conversation.

The jet fighter is a Grumman X-29. Its odd forward-swept wings enable it to be very agile in the air. There is a pilot in the cockpit, but without a robot system to balance the plane in flight, it would fall out of the sky.

High above, a Boeing E3A watches the battle. The big radar system in front of the tail gives the computer operators aboard details of everything that moves below.

1 Mini-Missile. A future weapon of the 1990s.
2 Superfly is already used in army units.
3 The X-29 prototype is due for flight in late 1983.
4 The E3A control plane is in service with the US Air Force. Several European countries have also ordered it.

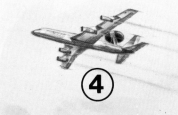

Robots to the stars

Just as robots are exploring the Solar System, so one day they may journey to the stars.

According to some experts, a starship could be built within the next hundred years. Compared to travel within the Solar System, distances are vast. A trip to Barnard's Star, a near neighbor of the Sun, would take 50 years, even cruising at a fantastic 22,400 miles per second (36,000 km/sec)!

In charge of the voyage is a robot. It controls the ship and has teams of wardens and probes. The wardens are mobile repair robots. They patrol the huge craft, keeping everything in working order.

As the ship nears Barnard's Star, the probes are launched to inspect any planets. Their findings are sent to the robot, which relays the information back to the scientists on Earth.

▷ In deep space, with Barnard's Star glowing ahead, a warden goes out to repair a broken power cable. In the weightless conditions of the flight, no legs or wheels are needed. Small gas jets are used to get around. The repair robot has four tool-equipped arms and a supply of spare parts.

Glossary

Here is a list of some of the technical words used in this book.

Android
A robot made to look like a human being. A cyborg is another robot-like creation. Like Steve Austin in the *Six Million Dollar Man* TV series, cyborgs are a marriage of living creature and machine parts. No one has yet made a real cyborg unless you count people with artificial hearts or limbs.

Computer
A machine that can take in information, process it according to a program of instructions, then tell you the answer to the problem.

Manganese nodule
Potato-shaped metallic lumps found scattered on the ocean floors around the world. Some are rich in minerals and may be worth mining.

Nuclear industry
Industries that work with nuclear power, which is produced by changing nuclei, the central parts of atoms.

Program
The set of instructions given to, and stored by, a robot or computer. The machine's operation depends entirely on this. Any new instructions are fed in as a new program – this is called reprogramming.

Radioactive
Some minerals, such as uranium, give off invisible rays. In large doses these rays – radioactivity – can be deadly.

Robot
Machine which can perform some of the movements of a human or animal. Robots are designed with simple jobs in mind, and today's robots rarely look anything like a human being.

Shakey
The first complete robot system, made in 1968. It could move around, see through a TV camera and detect objects when it bumped against them. It could push boxes together in groups according to instructions. Shakey was so-named because it wobbled as it rolled along.

Solar System
The planets, moons, asteroids and comets which move around the Sun. Outward from the Sun, the planets are: Mercury, Venus, Earth, Mars, Jupiter, Saturn, Uranus, Neptune, Pluto.

Strain gauge
Device which measures how much push or pull is being applied to an object. Used in robot

hands when they need to handle delicate objects.

Trip computer
Chip-controlled gadget found in lots of cars. It tells you how much fuel you are using, when you can expect to arrive at your destination, and so on.

Unimate
One of the most popular industrial robots. Made by Unimation Inc., which in 1972 became the first firm in the world to specialize in making robots.

Viking
Robot explorer which landed on Mars in 1976. There were two Viking missions, and in each case an orbiter stayed in space while a lander touched down on the surface. They took photographs and searched for life. A scoopful of martian soil was inspected in each lander's biological laboratory. No clear signs of life were discovered, though some scientists still think there may be life somewhere on Mars.

Robot facts

Here are some interesting facts about the world of robots.

The word robot comes from the Czech word "robota," meaning "to work."

The word was first used by Karel Capek. In 1920 he wrote a play called *R.U.R. (Rossum's Universal Robots)*. In the play android slave workers turn on their creators and kill them.

Japan first imported an American-made robot in 1967. Japan is now the robot center of the world.

The Wabot robot walks and talks. Its first two steps took nearly two minutes to complete, but it improved rapidly. Its inventor, Ichiro Kato, thinks that in the next 20 years, robots will take over many everyday jobs.

If the automobile had developed at the same rate as computers, a Rolls-Royce would sell for less than three dollars. Six cars would fit on a pinhead.

American robot sales are booming. The $100 million sales of 1980 are expected to jump to over $2 billion by 1990.

Orator is a talking typewriter developed for blind people. It senses the words typed into it, compares them with its memory store, then speaks the word. It also checks how to say the word properly – the difference between *rough* and *bough* is well within its grasp.

Masked robots are used in Japan as sparring partners in the bamboo sword sport of kendo.

31

Index